Glennie Kindred

how to stay well the natural way

THE WOODEN BOOKS SERIES

Title	ISBN
THE ALCHEMIST'S KITCHEN *how to prepare the Philosopher's Stone, by Guy Ogilvy*	978 1904263 52 4
ALTERED STATES *a guide to mind, drugs and human culture by Dr. Ben Sessa*	978 1904263 85 2
AVEBURY *packed with old engravings, a guide to the site by Evelyn Francis*	978 1904263 15 9
BENDER HEAVEN *tips on how to build the perfect eco-home by Laugh*	978 1904263 69 2
A LITTLE BOOK OF COINCIDENCE *geometry and harmony in the solar system by John Martineau*	978 1904263 05 0
CALLANISH *and other megalithic sites of the Outer Hebrides by Gerald Ponting*	978 1904263 08 1
CARNAC *and other megalithic sites in Southern Brittany by Howard Crowhurst*	978 1904263 96 8
CATHEDRALS *of ancient foundation in England, by Mark Mills*	978 1904263 41 8
ANCIENT CELTIC COIN ART *the lost world of a beautiful miniature tradition by Simon Lilly*	978 1904263 65 4
CELTIC PATTERN *visual rhythms of the ancient mind, by Adam Tetlow*	978 1904263 70 8
CHARMS, AMULETS, TALISMANS & SPELLS *an introduction to Magic, by Marian Gree*	978 1904263 89 0
THE COMPACT COSMOS *a small guide to the very big things, by Matt Tweed*	978 1904263 42 5
CROP CIRCLES *modern art without the artists by Michael Glickman*	978 1904263 34 0
CURVES *flowers, foliates and flourishes, by Lisa DeLong*	978 1904263 88 3
THE DIAGRAM *the geometry of harmony by Adam Tetlow*	978 1907155 33 8
DIVINATION *elements of wisdom by Jewels Rocka*	978 1904263 84 5
DOWSING *a guide to subtle skills by master dowser Hamish Miller*	978 1904263 53 1
A LITTLE HISTORY OF DRAGONS *the essential dragonologist's guide, by Joyce Hargreaves*	978 1904263 48 7
EARTH GRIDS *the secret patterns of Gaia's sacred sites, by Hugh Newman*	978 1904263 64 7
ANCIENT EARTHWORKS OF WESSEX *Neolithic, Iron Age and Roman by Gerald Ponting*	978 1904263 97 5
ESSENTIAL ELEMENTS *a fantastic guide to the Periodic Table, by Matt Tweed*	978 1904263 58 6
ETHICS *the art of character, by Gregory Beabout & Mike Hannis*	978 1904263 93 7
EUPHONICS *the magical qualities of phonetic sounds, by John Michell*	978 1904263 43 2
EVOLUTION *a little history of a great idea, by Gerard Cheshire*	978 1904263 80 7
FENG SHUI *secrets of Chinese geomancy, by Richard Creightmore*	978 1904263 86 9
FRACTALS *on the edge of chaos, by Oliver Linton*	978 1904263 98 2
GLASTONBURY *a guide to the Isle of Avalon by George Wingfield*	978 1904263 19 7
THE GOLDEN SECTION *in art, mathematics and nature, by Prof Scott Olsen*	978 1904263 47 0
GRAMMAR *the structure of language, by Rachel Grenon*	978 1904263 68 5
HARMONOGRAPH *a visual guide to the mathematics of music, by Anthony Ashton*	978 1904263 36 4
A HEDGEROW COOKBOOK *mouth-watering ways to stay alive, by Glennie Kindred*	978 1904263 03 6
HERBAL HEALERS *how to heal yourself the old-fashioned way, by Glennie Kindred*	978 1904263 01 2
THE HUMAN BODY *a beautiful guide to how you fit together, by Dr Moff Betts*	978 1904263 37 1
IRELAND'S HOLY HILLS & PAGAN PLACES *a guide for the Irish traveller, by Hector McDonnell*	978 1904263 03 6
IRISH ROUND TOWERS *a puzzle solved, by Hector McDonnell*	978 1904263 31 9
ISLAMIC DESIGN *the bestselling little introduction, by Daud Sutton*	978 1904263 59 3
LEYS *secret spirit paths of ancient Britain, by Danny Sullivan*	978 1904263 38 8
LI - DYNAMIC FORM IN NATURE *the art that nature chooses at every scale, by David Wade*	978 1904263 54 8
LIPSMACKING BACKPACKING *how to cook scrummily anywhere on Earth, by Mark Pallis*	978 1904263 57 9
LITERARY DEVICES *the essential book of tricks for writers, by Amy Jones*	978 1904263 06 7

First published 1999

Published by Wooden Books Ltd.
Glastonbury, Somerset

British Library Cataloguing in Publication Data
Kindred, G.
A Hedgerow Cookbook

A CIP catalogue record for this book
may be obtained from the British Library

ISBN-10: 1-904263-01-1
ISBN-13: 978-1-904263-01-2

Designed and typeset in Glastonbury, UK.

Printed in China on 100% FSC
approved sustainable papers by FSC
RR Donnelley Asia Printing Solutions Ltd.

HERBAL HEALERS

written & illustrated by

Glennie Kindred

For my children Jerry, Jack and May
and to my partner, Brian Boothby.

My thanks to the plant kingdom for their constant and abundant gifts to humankind, and to Brian Boothby for his invaluable support and advice.

May we remember to recognise that healing takes place on many levels. As herbs affect and heal our bodies, they also affect and heal our emotions and minds through the integration of their vital energy on many subtle levels of our being.

Contents

INTRODUCTION

THE WILD PLANTS AND HERBS of our land have long been used for their medical properties. They are our inherent connection to nature and aid our own effective ability and power to help ourselves when we are ill, instead of relying on costly, harsh, chemically produced drugs, which often have harmful side effects. Herbal remedies have been verified by modern scientific methods to have effective and deep acting properties.

Working with herbs is a participatory process from growing the herbs in your garden, or collecting herbs from the wild, to drying the herbs and making herbal preparations. Gardening takes on a new dimension as you harvest your 'weeds' for future medication, add helpful herbs to salads, or concoct your own herb teas. You can, of course, buy the ready dried herbs and herbal preparations from your local health shop.

I have chosen familiar, common and easy to recognise herbs, which can be used safely for a variety of common ailments and First Aid situations. Choose to work with the herbs you are naturally drawn towards, tuning into the plant and its subtle energy. Knowledge will grow as you use the herbs as a system and as you try things out and observe the results for yourself. However, should the symptoms persist or worsen, a trained medical herbalist or doctor should be consulted.

GENERAL CONSIDERATIONS

an ancient system

The traditional European system of medical astrology links each herb to one of the planets - Sun ☉ , Moon ☽ , Mercury ☿ , Venus ♀ , Mars ♂ , Jupiter ♃ and Saturn ♄ ; and to the four elements of Air 🜁 (digestion), Fire △ (attraction), Water ▽ (expulsion) and Earth 🜃 (retention). These are expressed as personality characteristics known as the four humours.

Sanguine: Air types 🜁. Hot and Moist. Expansive, communicative, quick-thinking and intuitive. Ruled by Jupiter ♃ (growth, dispersion, nutrition, the liver, fat cells and blood plasma).

Choleric: Fire types △. Hot and Dry. Energetic, passionate, enthusiastic and inspired. Ruled by the Sun ☉ (the vital spirit, heart and circulation) and Mars ♂ (red blood cells, gall bladder).

Phlegmatic: Water types ▽. Cold and Moist. Emotional, deep, feeling, psychic and sensitive. Ruled by the Moon ☽ (fluids, lymph glands and menstruation) and Venus ♀ (kidneys and reproduction).

Melancholic: Earth types 🜃. Cold and Dry. Careful, analytical, slow to react and liking boundaries. Ruled by Saturn ♄ (bones, teeth, skin and spleen) and Mercury ☿ (brain, nervous system, reflexes, thyroid and breathing).

Herbs are absorbed in teas, herbal salads or through the skin. They balance the humours, restoring equilibrium. Herbs which specifically strengthen and tone certain organs or systems can be used as a preventative medicine before any illness manifests itself.

DOSAGE

time and quantity

Many medicinal leaves, flowers and seeds can be eaten raw in salads, or straight off the plant, but it is more usual to take them in the form of herbal teas, taken 3 times a day.

Recipes are usually given in amounts of dried herb, because of their all year round availability, but it is always good to use a freshly picked herb which still holds the vibrant vital energy of the plant. Dried herbs do have a concentrated strength, so larger amounts of the fresh herb are needed.

1 teasp dried herb (5 ml) = 3 teasp or 1 tablesp of fresh herb.

For young people, the weak and the very elderly, halve the amount of herb.

The herbs in this book have been chosen for their safe, easy-to-recognise qualities. It would be hard to confuse them with any other plant which might be poisonous and it would be hard to overdose with any of these herbs; the worse that could happen is a headache, stomach ache or diarrhoea. A responsible and common sense approach is always vital when using herbal remedies.

Large doses do not necessarily work better; in fact the reverse is sometimes true, as subtler energies are released which affect the body on other levels. Modern medicine works on the assumption that we need instant results, but a slower healing process allows for greater understanding of the illness, bringing changes in lifestyle, diet and attitude, which will aid the effectiveness of the herbal treatment.

Generally it is not recommended to use a herb or a combination

of herbs for more than 12 weeks, because of the dangers of certain chemicals building up in the body.

Most minor conditions will improve within a few days and chronic problems within several weeks. As soon as the condition shows signs of improvement, gradually reduce the amount of herb until you feel you no longer need the remedy. Professional advice should be sought if there is no improvement after 8–12 weeks, or if there is a deterioration in the condition.

Herbal Preparations
for internal use

Herbal teas are prepared either as an infusion or as a decoction. Keep a special teapot for this, and make the tea in the spirit of positive awareness and thanks for the Earth's gifts. You will be surprised how much this open-hearted attitude will help in the healing process.

Infusion or Tisane (Soft ariel parts, leaves and flowers)

Use between half and one ounce (15 g-25 g) of the dried herb to one pint (570ml) of water. Two to three times more *fresh* herb is needed. Pour boiling water over the herb; cover, to keep in the essential oils, and leave to infuse for ten minutes. Strain off the herb.

Drink a cupful three times a day before meals for chronic conditions (which develop slowly over a long period) or every hour for acute illnesses (which come on suddenly and intensely). This brew will keep for two to three days if kept covered in the fridge. I like to drink it chilled in a wine glass, but it can be gently reheated (without boiling), with a spoonful of honey to sweeten.

Single dose: One teasp of dried herb to one cup (225 ml) of water.

Decoction (bark, roots, seeds and leaves)

Method One: The hard woody parts of plants need a greater heat before they can impart their properties into water. Chop or crush the bark, roots or seeds; use the same proportions as for infusions, and place all ingredients in a saucepan (not aluminium). Bring to the boil, cover, and simmer for ten to fifteen minutes. When cool, pour the unstrained liquid into a glass or pottery jug, and keep covered in the

fridge. Dosage is the same as an infusion.

Method Two: Using the same proportions as an infusion, pour cold water onto the leaves, and let them stand overnight. This will produce a strong solution.

Honey Syrup (for children)

Less palatable herbs can be flavoured with honey or a suitable aromatic herb. Bring slowly to the boil one pint of the infusion or decoction of herbs, with two to four tablespoons of honey, until the mixture turns syrupy. Strain and keep cool for up to two weeks.

HERBAL PREPARATIONS

for external use

The body readily absorbs herbs through the skin. A remedy can be given externally as well as internally.

Compresses or Fomentations

Apply a hot compress directly to the afflicted area. Use a clean cotton cloth, and soak it in a hot herbal infusion. Place this as hot as possible on the affected area. Redip it in the hot liquid as it cools. The heat activates the herb. To keep in the heat cover with a towel and a hot water bottle to keep it warm.

Poultices

Poultices are much like a compress but use the plant itself. Crush or mash the fresh or dried herb in a bowl with a little boiling water. Apply directly onto the skin, with a small amount of olive oil or thin muslin to protect the skin and help removal of the herb. Keep hot like a compress. Poultices are more active than compresses and are used to stimulate circulation, soothe aches and pains, or for drawing out impurities.

Baths

A wonderful way to absorb herbs through the skin is in the bath. Pour one pint of a strong herbal infusion or decoction into the bath water, and soak in it for ten to thirty minutes. The essential oils are absorbed through the skin and inhaled. For a foot bath pour the infusion into a bowl of water and soak the feet for 10-30 minutes.

Herbal Oils (macerations)

When rubbed onto the skin, herbal oils will be absorbed into the bloodstream and the herb will act in its usual way.

Half a pint (570ml) of Grapeseed or Almond oil.

3 oz (50g) of fresh herb, bruised between two stones (*or 1 oz dried*).

Mix the two together and place in a covered glass jar in a sunny position for one month, shaking daily. Alternatively, stand the jar in a double boiler and simmer for four hours. Strain off the herbs by pressing through muslin, and store in dark, well-sealed bottles. Extra virgin Olive oil may be used but it is less easily absorbed by the skin.

Collecting and Drying

tips and advice

Herbs are best collected on a sunny morning after the dew has dried. Choose the finest plants, growing in big clumps away from roads or sprayed land. Do not deplete the area. Pick randomly and instinctively and leave plenty of flowers for propagation.

Gather and dry those leaves, flowers, seeds, berries and roots which you think will be the most useful to you later in the year - for winter colds and First Aid, those for reoccurring weakness and problems, and also herbal tonics and preventatives. Take a basket, or brown paper bags. Do not pack them tightly or over-handle.

Harvest your herbs when their power is at its optimum peak. If you miss this point they can still be harvested and dried, or used fresh, but may not be so strong. All herbs can be bought dried from health food shops when needed. Leaves are at their prime just before the flowers open. Flowers are at their prime just as they open. Roots are best picked in Autumn when the goodness is passed back down from the leaves. Pick the aerial parts of the herbs as the moon is waxing to full and the roots as the moon is waning. I like to thank the plants as I am picking them, affirming my use for the herb.

Dry the herbs in a warm dry airy place away from direct sunlight, hanging them in bunches, or laying them out on clean sheets of paper. Turn them frequently. Drying times vary, but the stems and stalks should snap cleanly. Roots should be washed (not soaked), chopped and laid out to dry. They should be dry enough to snap or chip with a hammer.

Direct sunlight weakens dried herbs so store them in brown paper or darkened jars. Keep them dry and label them carefully. Dried herbs should smell and taste as good as the fresh plant, discard them if they smell musty. Leaves and flowers will last for about a year. Fruit, roots and bark will last for up to two years.

Dried herbs can be used in salads, cooking, drinks and baths, as well as in medicine. They can also be used in pot pourri, tussie-mussies (fragrant posies with symbolic meanings and hidden messages), garlands, wreaths, hangings and herb sachets and pillows. The dried aromatic leaves, seeds, flowers and berries can be burnt as incense, their subtle properties released for invocation and ritual.

BRAMBLE

rubus fruticosus

Bramble also goes by the name of Blackberry, Brambleberry, Scaldhead, Bumble Kite, Cloudberry, Dewberry and Thimbleberry. Harvest the buds, the pink-white flowers and the leaves in July and August.

An infusion of blackberry or bramble leaves taken internally is a general tonic and blood cleanser, and will help with anaemia, general debility and diarrhoea. This same mixture can be used externally on wounds, sores, burns and scalds.

Chewing fresh blackberry leaves has long been used to relieve bleeding gums and general sores in the mouth.

A decoction of the leaves or root applied externally will help clear up skin problems such as blemishes, blackheads and itchy scalps.

Other species of Rubus like raspberries and loganberries have the same properties. Blackberries are a good source of vitamin C. In the past the bramble was a popular charm herb, used for binding spells, and for containing energy.

If drunk as a herbal tea it will enhance the qualities of persistence and patience, both in love and spiritual discipline, bringing sweetness as an end result (its symbolic role in the Sleeping Beauty story).

Nerve tonic - Blood cleanser - Skin problems

Burns - Wounds - Anaemia - Diarrhoea

CHAMOMILE

anthemis nobilis

Also known as Roman Chamomile, Manzanilla (Spanish for 'little apple'), Maythen, Common Chamomile, Ground Apple and Kamai (Greek), the white flowers have a yellow centre; harvest them with the leaves in July and August.

An infusion of the flowers and leaves is an ideal tonic for children, healing nervous excitability, anxiety and insomnia. The same infusion relieves toothache, earache, indigestion and headaches due to gastric disturbances. It can also be used as a mouthwash for gingivitis, for bathing inflamed or sore eyes, as a gargle for sore throats, for wound healing and to reduce swellings. It can additionally be used as a poultice.

Chamomile has a beneficial effect on the womb, and can be used for PMT, menstrual cramps, to regulate menstrual periods and to ease the pain of childbirth.

Bathing in a decoction will take away weariness. An oil made from the flowers is good for aches and pains in the joints or any part of the body, and for hard swellings.

Chamomile quietens, relaxes and centres a person. Use it whenever you need to feel nourished and nurtured. It can be used safely with babies (it is good for colic), children and the elderly.

Calming - Anti inflammatory - Antiseptic
Analgesic (pain killer) - Wound healer
Gastric disturbances - Beneficial to the Womb

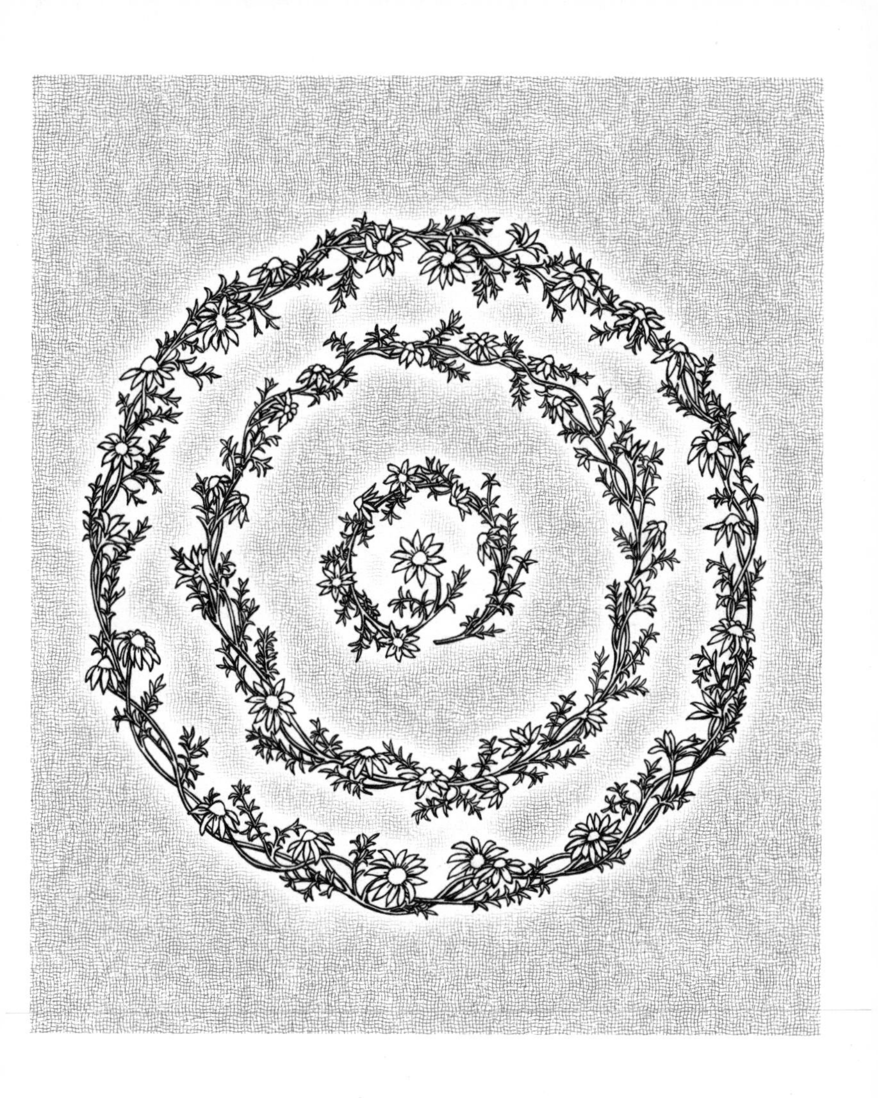

CHICKWEED

stellaria media

Other names for Chickweed include Starweed, Starwort, Adder's Mouth, Tongue Grass, Satin Flower and Stellaire (French). Its small star-like flowers appear all year round. Harvest the flowers and leaves from June to August.

A supreme healer, whether used externally or internally, chickweed can be eaten raw in salads or as a spinach. Use an infusion of the leaves to soothe all inflammations of the digestive system, including stomach ulcers, colitis, cramps. It has an affinity to the lungs, and is helpful for bronchitis, pleurisy, coughs and hoarseness.

For rheumatism, use both internally and externally. Use internally for blood poisoning and for cleansing the whole system.

Chickweed is a healing demulcent (soothes inflamed tissue), and has remarkable drawing powers, absorbing impurities from the skin to heal boils, abscesses, wounds and sores and eczema. Apply the plant directly on the skin, cover with a large leaf from a cabbage, lettuce or geranium, and bind with a cotton bandage. Change the chickweed every three hours. It is also good for irritating skin problems like heat rash.

This herb enhances compassion and receptivity, and is helpful for people who are too self-contained and controlled.

Healing - Soothing and cooling to the Skin
Digestive System - Lungs and Blood
Draws out Poisons

☽

Cleavers

galium aparine

Cleavers is also known as Sticky Willy, Goosegrass, Catchweed, Hedgeriff, Hayriffe, Robin-run-in-the-grass, Bedstraw, Goosebill, Grip Grass, Love-man, Everlasting Friendship, Clivers and Tongebledes. The stems and fruit catch on clothes and animal fur. Pick the flowers and leaves in June and July.

Taken as an infusion, cleavers is a prime blood purifier and an important spring tonic. It is a deep acting cleanser and diuretic, which will strengthen and stimulate the lymphatic system and hence improve the immune system and fluid balance. Take an infusion of cleavers for a few weeks after viral infections, antibiotic drugs, chemotherapy, steroids and anti-depressants.

This is the remedy for long lasting viral infections and for any disease of the lymphatic system where there are swollen glands, such as mumps, tonsillitis and so on. The infusion will soothe all mucus membranes, reducing inflammation in the mouth, gut, vagina and bladder (cystitis). Used externally as well as internally it also benefits dry skin diseases such as psoriasis and dandruff. The crushed leaves can be applied directly onto sores and blisters. Also an old time tonic - added to beer.

Cleavers has a calming, soothing influence on the emotions, renewing strength and energy. Take before a change in direction.

Blood purifier - Tonic for the Lymphatic system
Immune system - Skin conditions - Cystitis

COLTSFOOT

tussilago farfara

Also known as The Son before the Father, Coughwort, Hall Foot, Horse Foot, Ass's Foot, Foal's Foot, Fieldhove, Bull's Foot and Country Tobacco Plant. Coltsfoot leaves are green on top, and white and furry underneath. The flowers appear first and can be picked in February, harvest the leaves in March and April.

Coltsfoot has a beneficial effect on the respiratory system. The infusion of flowers or leaves will soothe dry coughs and help dry up phlegm. It is a decongestant (colds) and a relaxant, useful for asthma and breathlessness. The zinc it contains will heal any damaged or diseased tissue and has a marked anti-inflammatory effect. It is soothing to the throat and larynx and will help tonsillitis, laryngitis and bronchitis.

If you are a smoker, allergic to dust, or cycle or walk in the city, drink coltsfoot tea regularly to help clear the lungs of tar, dust and other pollutants. Coltsfoot can be dried and smoked as a herbal tobacco which can occasionally have a beneficial effect on the lungs!

The crushed leaves or a decoction can be applied directly onto insect bites, boils, inflammations, burns or ulcers.

Coltsfoot tea can be drunk to help clear the vibrational channels, to help enhance clairvoyance and for receiving messages. It may also be burnt as an incense.

Lungs - Coughs - Respiratory problems
External skin problems

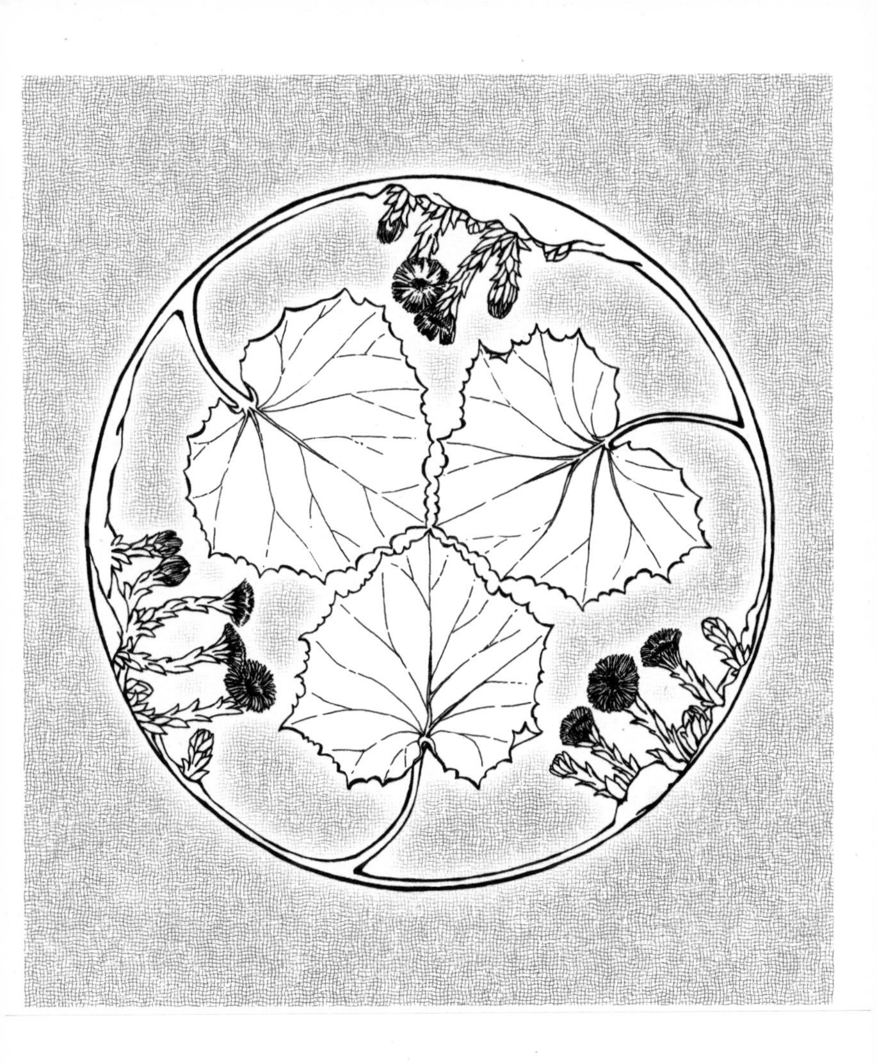

DANDELION

taraxacum officinale

Also known as Piss-in-the-bed, Devil's Milk-pail, Priest's Crown, Blow Ball, Cankerwort, Lion's Tooth, Wild Endive and Swine's Snout, Dandelion has yellow flowers which only open fully in the sunshine. Collect aerial parts from May to August, roots November to March.

Eaten raw in a salad or taken as an infusion, dandelion leaves act as a blood cleanser and lymph tonic, removing poisons from the system. It is helpful for all deep-seated chronic infections and viruses, for arthritis and rheumatism.

Dandelion leaf is *the* remedy for kidney and bladder complaints, like cystitis. The root is useful for all diseases of the liver (hepatitis and jaundice), and for helping the body digest fatty foods. It is good for relieving constipation.

It has also long been used as an effective treatment for duodenal and stomach ulcers. Dandelion root helps the blood in the veins circulate and therefore is helpful in treating varicose veins and haemorrhoids (or as a preventative). Split the stems and rub the juice onto bee stings, warts, blisters and old sores.

This is a very useful herb for emotional stagnation, turning depression into expression and self-empowerment.

Warning: Do not use if there are kidney stones.

Blood cleanser - Lymph tonic - Kidneys
Liver - Stomach - Arthritis

♃

ELDERFLOWER

sambucus nigra

Also known as Ellhorn, Ellanwood, Bore Tree, Pipe Tree, Rob Elder, Hylder, Hylan Tree, Eldrum, Elhorn, Hollunder, Sureau and Queen-of-Trees, Elderflowers are small, creamy-white and musty smelling; harvest them in May and June, and the leaves all summer.

Make an infusion of the flowers as an excellent daily spring tonic. Drink hot as a tea to promote perspiration in fevers and for expectoration of any excess mucus in the head or lungs. Elderflower will help any catarrhal inflammations like hayfever, sinusitis, catarrhal deafness and coughs.

Elderflowers are a sedative and can be drunk before bed to promote a peaceful sleep. The flowers can also be used externally as an excellent skin tonic and along with the leaves can be used on wounds, bruises, sprains, burns and scalds. Rub the fresh leaves on the skin as an insecticide.

A lotion can be made by pouring boiling water on the blossoms. Infuse for an hour and then strain. This can be used for cooling and soothing the skin, for rashes and particularly for bathing the eyes.

Elder is useful for the relief of 'stuck' emotionally congested states. It will help to move fears and bring clarity, easing worries and night fears. Drink as a tea before bed, or sleep with some flowers under your pillow. Grow near the house for protection and prosperity.

Specific for phlegm - Colds - Fevers - Catarrh
Sore eyes - Coughs - Skin tonic - Spring tonic

FENNEL

foeniculum vulgare

Other names for Fennel include Fenkel, Sweet Fennel and Marathon. Fennel has small yellow flowers which have a strong aniseed smell like all parts of the plant. Harvest the leaves during the summer and the seeds and bulbs in the Autumn.

The leaves and seeds are used for all gastric disturbances, stimulating digestion, reducing bloating and helping to expel wind. Drink as a refreshing tea after meals (especially the bruised seeds). Chewing the leaves or seeds will greatly relieve hunger pains and constipation. A slimming aid.

Fennel gets rid of cold and dampness. An infusion will help bronchitis, asthma or any lung condition where catarrh has accumulated. It soothes harsh and irritating coughs. A tea made from the bruised seeds can be safely drunk by nursing mothers to increase milk production, passing through the milk to the baby to reduce wind and colic. It is the main ingredient of gripe water.

The fresh juice of the leaves has long been used for clearing the eyesight if misty, and a decoction of the roots and leaves will neutralise vegetable poisons (from mushrooms etc.).

Use this nourishing and sustaining plant whenever you need to be nurtured. It calms and soothes the emotions, loosening sensuality.

Warning: Uterine stimulant. Use sparingly when pregnant.

Digestive tonic – Lung remedy

Gastric Disturbances

GARLIC

allium sativum

Sometimes also called Poor Mans Treacle, Heal All or Theriac, unearth the bulbs of cloves in September when the leaves first wither.

Garlic is a remarkable herb which will aid the body on many levels. It can be used as a preventative for most diseases of the digestive, respiratory and circulatory systems. Eat two to three cloves of garlic daily (preferably raw).

Garlic will aid the development of natural bacterial flora, whilst killing pathogenic organisms. It can be used for all viral and fungal infections, colds and fevers. It is also good for respiratory problems, chronic bronchitis, respiratory catarrh, whooping cough and asthma.

It will help in all circulation and heart problems, causing blood pressure to be lowered, as well as helping reduce blood cholesterol levels, and angina. It is a good external rub for arthritic and rheumatic pain when used hot.

The juice diluted with water, or mashed as a poultice, may be applied directly onto wounds. It is an antiseptic and anti-infective with drawing properties.

Garlic makes it easier to transcend the physical plane, thus aiding astral travel and even the transition of death.

Antiseptic - Digestive system - Lungs
Colds - Heart and circulation
Viral and fungal infections

HAWTHORN

crataegus monogyna

Hawthorn is also known as May Tree, May Quick, Quickthorn, Whitethorn, Haw, Hagthorn, Bread and Cheese Tree, or just 'Thorn'. The berries go by the names of Pixie Pears, Cuckoo Beads, Chucky Cheese and Ladies Meat. The May flowers are white or pink and have a strong heady smell; harvest them with the leaves through to June. The deep red berries are picked in October.

A herbal decoction of hawthorn berries is the primary remedy for all problems of the heart. Drunk regularly as a pleasant tea, it relieves palpitations, angina, hardening of the arteries, water retention and poor circulation. It will regulate high or low blood pressure, depending on the need, and gently brings the heart to normal function, improving its general condition.

It is safe to take this excellent herb regularly in old age, and for any nervous conditions including stress and insomnia.

A poultice of the pulped berries and/or leaves has strong drawing powers, and has long been used for embedded thorns, splinters and whitlows.

Hawthorn releases blocked subtle energies, opening the heart to giving and receiving love. By releasing stress it enhances the person's ability to let go and trust. Use to heal broken hearts.

Heart conditions - Circulation

Nervous conditions - Regulates the heart

Draws out splinters

Hops

humulus lupulus

Also known as Hop Vine, Beer Plant and Lupulus, this perennial hedgerow climber has vine-like leaves. Gather the female scaly green flowers before they are fully ripe in August/September, drying them carefully in the shade.

An infusion of Hop flowers can be used as a mild sedative tea, for digestive problems, and as an appetite stimulant. It has a marked relaxing effect on the central nervous system, relieving tensions and anxiety, especially where this causes headaches, indigestion, irritable bowels, duodenal ulcers and restlessness. An anti-aphrodisiac.

A prime remedy in the treatment of insomnia and nightmares, Hop pillows can be made each year by filling a small cotton pillow case with crushed hop flowers and a handful of Lavender flowers. Alternatively, drink an infusion of the flowers at night before bed.

Make a poultice of hop flowers to help abscesses and boils come to a head and for the treatment of itchy skin conditions, sores and wounds. As a painkiller, hops can be used to relieve toothache and earache. The flowers may also be eaten raw or mixed with honey.

Hops increase urine flow and reduce water retention, cleansing the kidneys of stones, and the bloodstream of poisons. It reduces anxiety, irritability and restlessness. Good for adolescence.

Warning: Do not use if you feel depressed.

Insomnia - Nervous conditions - Sores

Toothache - Earache - Kidneys - Ulcers

Lavender

lavendula officinalis

Also known as Stickadore, Spikenard, Nard, Nardus, Asarum and Elf Leaf, the small purple flowers are harvested from June to August.

Lavender is a gentle strengthening tonic for the nervous system. Make an infusion of the flowers for states of nervous debility and exhaustion, insomnia, physical and mental tension, and migraines and headaches related to stress and the sun. It prevents fainting and allays nausea and travel sickness.

Use lavender as a tea and in baths for easing the aches and pains of rheumatism and any general weakness of the limbs. Externally, use as a mouthwash for infected gums and mouth ulcers, insect bites, infections and sunburn.

It cleanses the bloodstream of toxins, strengthening the liver and clearing stagnation. It also strengthens the stomach, reducing bloating and wind after meals, and lowers blood pressure, calming palpitations of the heart and hot flushes.

Lavender brings relaxation, deeper states of meditation, trance states and a oneness with all things. It helps bring spiritual understanding into everyday life. Use as an incense for cleansing, new beginnings, for connection to your potential and unformed ideas.

Warning: Do not use with insulin (diabetic). Avoid if epileptic.

Nervous debility - Exhaustion - Insomnia
Liver - Digestive stimulant - Antiseptic
Lowers blood pressure - Migraines

Lemon Balm

melissa officinalis

This herb also goes by the names of Sweet Balm, Balm Mint, Bee Balm, Cure All, Melissa, or just 'Balm'. The small white flowers are traditionally picked on midsummer's day but are available with the leaves from June to August.

Balm is an excellent calming herb which will soothe all digestive pains and upsets due to wind, tension and anxiety. It will help in the digestion of fatty foods. Try drinking an infusion of the leaves after a heavy meal to reduce bloating and discomfort.

The same infusion has a tonic effect on the heart and circulatory system, regulating the flow of blood round the body, helping to lower blood pressure. It is also a useful herb to take during the menopause, helping with hot flushes, depression, anxiety and palpitations. Taken regularly, melissa can regulate irregular menstruation and ease period pains. It is safe to use in pregnancy for headaches, dizziness and morning sickness.

The infusion will lower fevers and promote sweating in colds and flu, and bring relief from chronic bronchial catarrh and coughs. Rub the fresh leaves directly onto insect bites.

Balm drives away all troubles and cares, lifts the spirits and eases depression. It is soothing and expansive, opening the heart and increasing mental stamina, memory and calm focus.

Digestive system - Heart and circulation - Fevers
Menstruation - Menopause - Anti-depressant

♃

MARIGOLD

calendula officinalis

Also known as Golds, Ruddes, Mary Gowles, Oculus Christi, Pot Marigold and Mary Gold, the yellow to deep orange petals are picked June to August.

A powerful healing remedy, safe to use with babies and children. Use an infusion of the flowers internally and externally for varicose veins, eye infections (conjunctivitis), wounds in the digestive tract (ulcers or colitis) and for slow healing wounds.

Marigold flowers are a powerful blood cleanser (for boils, eczema, acne) and act on the lymphatic system (swollen lymph glands, tonsillitis). Take them whenever the immune system is lowered, and for viral and fungal infections (candida). The leaves and flowers can be eaten raw.

It is a potent liver remedy (jaundice, hepatitis) and helps relieve pre-menstrual tension by stimulating the action of the liver, thus speeding up the breakdown of hormones. It will regulate irregular menstruation, heal vaginal infections (especially thrush) and wounds caused by gynaecological surgery.

Calendula will bring comfort to the spirit. It has a soothing effect after shock, trauma or anger.

Warning: Avoid during pregnancy.

Immune system - Wounds - Sprains - Burns
Wasp and bee stings - Liver - Blood cleanser
Viral and fungal infections - Reproductive system

MEADOW SWEET

filipendula ulmaria

Other names for this herb include Meadsweet, Doll Off, Queen of the Meadows, Bridewort and Lady of the Meadow. The creamy yellow flowers have a distinctive smell and are picked with the leaves in July and August.

An infusion of Meadowsweet flowers reduces excess acidity in the stomach and the duodenum, protecting and soothing the mucus membranes of the digestive tract. Use for heartburn, hyper-acidity, gastritis and peptic ulcers. It cleanses the body of harmful acids and is used for any inflammatory condition (such as rheumatoid arthritis).

This is a strong diuretic (increases urine) which can be used for bladder and kidney complaints. It reduces stagnation in the liver and helps the immune system function more effectively. The flowers will bring out a really good sweat, lowering fevers. Use for childrens' infectious diseases (chickenpox, mumps, diarrhoea) and feverish colds. Also, take with honey for a pleasant diet drink.

Meadowsweet expands the psyche and builds inner strength, enhancing flexibility and alignment to divine purpose. Traditionally gathered for wedding garlands and posies.

Warning: Contains salicylic acid (aspirin) which affects the rate at which blood clots. Avoid if on anticoagulant drugs.

Mild sedative and painkiller - Fevers
Immune system - Inflammation - Arthritis
Diarrhoea (esp. children) - Ulcers

♃

NETTLE

urtica dioica & urens

Also known as Stinging Nettle, Common Nettle, and Netel, the hanging clusters of white flowers can be harvested with the dark green stinging leaves from May to September.

Regular infusions of nettle-leaf tea will tone up the whole body and cleanse the blood. Nettle is a powerful diuretic, increasing urination, and will clear the body of uric acid, thereby easing arthritis, rheumatism, stiff joints and failing muscular strength. It has long been used to soften and expel kidney stones.

It will relieve bronchial and asthmatic conditions, wheezing and catarrh, clearing the body of accumulated phlegm. Also take for anaemia or bloodloss. It is a good herb to take in late pregnancy; the high iron content will regulate haemoglobin levels and stimulate milk production.

A strong infusion or poultice of the fresh leaves can be used for burns and to arrest bleeding. The fresh juice will antidote its own sting. It can also be used as a hair rinse, and to remove dandruff. The fresh leaves and shoot tips can be picked in the spring and boiled and eaten as a vegetable or in soups.

Nettle is good if you need to get in touch with your fiery energy. Drink an infusion daily to break free of stagnant emotional states and to contact the warrior within. Use for protection against negativity.

Blood cleanser - Spring tonic - Wounds
Arthritis - Rheumatism - Stiffness - Asthma

ROSEMARY

rosemarinus officinalis

Other names for Rosemary include Polar Plant, Compass Weed, Rosmarine (rose of the sea), Incensier, Romero and The Pilgrims Flower. The small purple flowers can be collected and used with the dark needly leaves from May to September.

Rosemary leaves strengthen the heart and increase circulation. Drink the infusion as a preventative against hardening of the arteries. It helps with cold limbs, poor circulation and chilblains. It will raise low blood pressure.

Use as a stimulant for the whole system, when the body is sluggish or lethargic, and when there is a lack of concentration and a poor memory due to feeling cold. It is good for all nervous tensions and for headaches due to gastric disturbances and general debility. It is a liver and digestive remedy, relieving flatulence, colic and indigestion, and will help the body digest fatty or rich foods. Externally it may be used to ease muscular pains, neuralgia, on wounds, bites and stings, as an insecticide and as a hair rinse.

Rosemary lets joy and love into the heart, dispelling grief, anger, hatred and bitterness. It strengthens, warms and stimulates. A symbol of love and loyalty which also enhances creativity.

Warning: Do not take during pregnancy with high blood pressure.

Nervous system - Heart and circulation
Digestion and liver - Muscle pains - Blood pressure
Headaches - Wounds - Hair tonic - Insecticide

SAGE

salvia officinalis

Also known as Garden Sage, Sawge (*old English*), Salvia, Red Sage, White Sage and Sage the Saviour, the purple flowers appear from July onwards. The pale green leaves are best picked in July before the plant flowers.

Sage leaf tea can be drunk whenever there is a weakness in the liver, kidneys, heart and digestive systems. It is a valued fever cure. As an antiseptic it can be used as a gargle for sore throats, tonsillitis, laryngitis (swallowing the infusion afterwards) and for any mouth infections, inflamed or bleeding gums and mouth ulcers. It dries up excess secretions (sinusitis and catarrh) and is excellent as a steam inhalation. Used externally, it is good for any wounds, sores or ulcers and for stopping bleeding.

It contains oestrogen and, drunk hot, will bring on a delayed period and help in the treatment of hot flushes. Use with care, however, as it can be very drying (mouth, anus and vagina); it can even dry up mother's milk.

Sage is often associated with the throat and enhances verbal communication, also releasing and expressing emotions more easily.

Warning: Do not take large doses for long periods. Do not use during pregnancy. Avoid if insulin dependent or epileptic.

Liver, kidney and heart tonic - Digestive aid
Menstruation - Antiseptic - Excess secretions
Throat - Fevers - Wounds

♃

St John's Wort

hypericum perforatum

Also known as Hypericum, Klamath Weed, Amber, Goat Weed and Tipton Weed, harvest the yellow flowers with the leaves around midsummer.

The entire plant above ground is a valuable pain-reducing, anti-inflammatory and general healing remedy. St. John's Wort is used for the treatment of wounds, ulcers, blisters, shingles, herpes, bruises, rashes, varicose veins, minor burns and sunburn. Take internally at the same time as using externally. It is a wonderful remedy for the nervous system, an anti-depressant and sedative.

It is especially indicated where there are menopausal changes of irritability and anxiety. St. John's Wort makes an excellent healing, relaxing massage oil, especially good where there is tension, neuralgia, sciatica, fibrositis or rheumatic pains.

Use anywhere there is nerve irritation, pain, neuritis, neuralgia, tickly coughs and so on. It will clear congestion from the lungs, will suppress the flow of urine and can be used for bed-wetting in children - drink an infusion of the flowers and leaves before bed. Also used for dysentery, diarrhoea and worms.

St. John's Wort is very uplifting to the emotions, clearing fears and phobias and bringing peaceful sleep, as well as allowing the nervous system to heal. It will let light in and dispel darkness.

Sedative - Pain reducing - Wounds - Sunburn
Inflammations - Menopausal changes - Expectorant

Thyme

thymus vulgaris

Also known as Garden Thyme, Mother of Thyme, Thymus (from old Greek, meaning courage and also 'to fumigate'). Harvest the leaves together with the purple flowers from June to September.

The calming antiseptic qualities of Thyme make it a valuable tonic for the whole system. Make an infusion of the leaves for all digestive complaints including inflammation of the liver, nervous indigestion, flatulence, bad breath and hangovers. It is particularly good for kidney infections, stimulating white blood cell production to resist infection. An anti-fungal, use regularly for candida and thrush.

Thyme helps expel mucus from the lungs, purging the body of phlegm. Use for bronchitis, tonsillitis, pleurisy, septic sore throats, ear infections and dry irritating coughs. Used internally as well as externally it promotes perspiration in fevers, lowers the temperature and quickly cleanses the body. It will relieve insomnia and calm night fears. Add to the bath to throw off lethargy and chills.

Externally use a hot fomentation for abscesses, boils and all swellings. Use in the bath to alleviate the pains of rheumatism and all muscular pain. Use as a lotion for itchy skin and hives.

Thyme brings courage, inner strength and a stronger purpose. Use to attract good health and remove all sorrows from the past.

Antiseptic - Lungs - Liver - Kidneys - Digestive tonic
Candida - Sore throats - Ear infections - Fevers
Abscesses - Muscular pain

Yarrow

achillea millefolium

Other names for Yarrow include Milfoil (a thousand leaves), Nose Bleed, Old Man's Pepper, Soldier's Woundwort, Knight's Milfoil, Bloodwort, Staunch Weed, Sanguinary, Devil's Nettle, Devil's Plaything and Yarroway. Harvest the clusters of small white flowers with the dark feathery leaves from Midsummer to early Autumn.

One of the best fever remedies, Yarrow produces copious sweating, lowering the blood pressure. Take an infusion of the flowers and leaves in the bath, and also drink hourly until the fever subsides (combine with elderflower and peppermint).

Yarrow tones the blood vessels and aids digestion. It is a specific in thrombotic conditions associated with high blood pressure. It also contains a natural antiseptic which will ease cystitis. Use too for diarrhoea (safe with children).

It will speed up the clotting of blood and can be used for all wounds, old and new, rashes, haemorrhoids, and for checking over-profuse menstruation. It is a useful emergency treatment to check haemorrhaging. Use the crushed leaves directly on cuts, for nose bleeds or earache. Chew them for toothache. In China, yarrow stalks are used with the I Ching oracle system; in Europe, the Druids used yarrow to divine the weather.

Yarrow strengthens and protects the etheric body (the aura).

Fevers - Cold and flu - Digestive tonic - Menstruation
Urinary antiseptic - Diarrhoea - All wounds

OTHER USEFUL HERBS

BORAGE - ♃ ***borago officinalis***. *Borage is an excellent adrenal tonic and will revive and renew the adrenal glands after medical treatment, especially after using cortisone or steroids, or other stresses. A good herb for convalescence. The young tops can be boiled as a pot herb and the blue starry flowers used in salads. It drives away sorrows and increases joy in the mind.*

GINGER - ☉ ***zingiber officinale***. *A hot dry herb. Use the sliced root as a decoction for illnesses caused by the cold and wet. It is very good for poor circulation, arthritis, aching bones, menstrual cramps or shock. It will move heat from the head down to other parts of the body. It reduces water retention by increasing sweating.*

Warning: Do not use if there is heat in the body such as high blood pressure, inflammatory conditions, stomach ulcers.

HERB ROBERT - ♀ ***geranium robertianum***. *Like all Geraniums, it is a good wound herb with healing and drawing properties. Antiseptic. Make an infusion or apply fresh leaves bruised and bound in place. Relieves pain and inflammation. Drink the herbal infusion and bathe the wound directly. Useful for diabetics, it lowers blood sugar levels.*

SELF HEAL - ♀ ***prunella vulgaris***. *Gather the young shoots, leaves and purple flowers during the summer. Use the fresh leaf directly onto cuts and wounds or as a poultice or compress. Use the infusion externally and internally for sore throats, mouth ulcers and as a general strengthening tonic.*

SHEPHERDS PURSE - ♄ ***capsella bursa pastoris***. *A useful emergency First Aid which helps clot blood. An antiseptic, it will staunch the bleeding of wounds and nose bleeds. Use the fresh juice on cotton wool with a little cold water, or a strong infusion made with a dessert spoonful of the fresh herb to 1 cup of boiling water. Apply externally or internally for haemorrhages of all kinds, stomach, lungs, uterus or kidneys. Also useful for diarrhoea, cystitis, heavy menstruation, thrush and fibroids in the uterus.*

Warning: Do not take if pregnant.

Some Useful Trees

ALDER - ♀ ***alnus glutinosa***. *The leaves are cooling and soothing. Use them fresh inside your shoes when walking long distances to soothe aching burning feet. Pulp up a handful of leaves, moisten with warm milk and bind over any swellings.*

ASPEN - ♄ ***populus tremula***. *Use the buds, leaves or bark for all conditions relating to poor digestion. Also good for headaches, lethargy, debility or irritability. It contains salicylic acid, more commonly known as aspirin.*

BLACKTHORN - ♄ ***prunus spinosa***. *Blackthorn flowers make a reliable and harmless purgative with beneficial effects on the stomach. Helps stimulate the appetite.*

CRAB APPLE - ♀ ***malus sylvestris*** *(including cultivated apple trees). The fruit is a tonic and cleanser which aids digestion. Peeled and grated it is excellent for diarrhoea. A decoction made with the dried peel is recommended for rheumatism.*

LINDEN or COMMON LIME - ♃ ***tilia x vulgaris***. *Harvest the flowers in midsummer to make a pleasant herbal tea. To calm and tone the whole nervous system, for indigestion, hysteria, stress, nervous vomiting, palpitations, to soothe the tensions of PMT, for gastric and duodenal ulcers (stomach). Warning: Avoid using old flowers as they may produce mild intoxication.*

ROWAN - ☿ ***sorbus aucuparia***. *Harvest the berries in September. Make a decoction and use the juice as a mild laxative. It makes a good gargle for sore throats and hoarseness.*

SILVER BIRCH - ♀ ***betula pendula***. *Collect the young leaves in late spring. Antiseptic, diuretic and tonic. For cystitis, arthritis and rheumatism.*

WILLOW - ☽ ***salix nigra***. *Willow bark contains salicylic acid (aspirin) and can be used for headaches and pains just like aspirin. Good for circulation problems, as a gargle for sore throats, and a mouthwash for mouth ulcers. It eliminates toxins from the body.*

REPERTORY

specifics highlighted - abbreviations listed below

Ald - Alder (p.55)
Bla - Blackthorn (p.55)
Bra - Bramble (p.12)
Cha - Chamomile (p.14)
Chi - Chickweed (p.16)
Cle - Cleavers (p.18)
Col - Coltsfoot (p.20)
Cra - Crab Apple (p.55)
Dan - Dandelion (p.22)
Eld - Elder (p.24)
Fen - Fennel (p.26)
Gar - Garlic (p.28)
Gin - Ginger (p.54)
Haw - Hawthorn (p.30)
Hon - Honeysuckle (p.54)
Hop - Hops (p.32)
Lav - Lavender (p.34)
Lem - Lemon Balm (p.36)
Lin - Linden/Lime (p.55)
Mar - Marigold (p.38)
Mea - Meadowsweet (p.40)
Net - Nettle (p.42)
Rob - Herb Robert (p.54)
Ros - Rosemary (p.44)
Row - Rowan (p.55)
Sag - Sage (p.46)
StJ - St Johns Wort (p.48)
Sel - Self Heal (p.54)
She - Shepherds Purse (p.54)
Sil - Silver Birch (p.55)
Thy - Thyme (p.48)
Yar - Yarrow (p.52)
Wil - Willow (p.55)

Abscess	*Chi, Col,* ***Gar****, Thy, Hop*
Aching bones	*Gin*
Acidity	*Col, Lem,* ***Mea****, Net*
Acne	***Cle****, Gar, Mar*
Adenoids	***Cle, Gar, Mar***
Anaemia	*Bra,* ***Net***
Angina pectoris	***Gar, Haw***
Antiseptics	*Cha, Gar, Hon, Rob, Ros,* ***Sag****, Sil,* ***Thy****, Yar*
Anxiety	*Hop,****Cha****, Lav, Lem,* ***StJ***
Appetite	*Hop, Bla*
Arthritis	*Dan, Gin, Hon* ***Mea****, Net, Sil, Thy*
Asthma	*Cha, Col, Fen, Gar, Hon, Lem, Net, Sag*
Athlete's foot	***Mar, Gar***
Bed wetting	*StJ*
Bladder infections	***Dan****,Mea,Yar*
Bleeding	***Mar****, Net, Sag,* ***She****, Yar*
Blisters	*Cle, Dan, StJ*
Blood cleansers	*Bra, Chi,* ***Cle****,* ***Dan****, Lav, Mar,Mea,* ***Net****, Sag*
Blood poisoning	*Chi,* ***Dan****, Net*
Blood pressure	***Gar, Haw****, Lav, Lem, Mea, Ros, Yar*
Boils	*Cle, Chi,Col,Hop* ***Gar****, Hop, Mar, Thy*
Broken Bones	*Com*
Bronchitis	*Chi,* ***Col****, Fen,* ***Gar****, Lem, Net, StJ*
Bruises	*Eld, Mar, StJ*
Burns	*Bra, Cha, Chi, Col,* ***Eld, Mar****, Net,* ***StJ***
Candida	*Thy, Mar*
Catarrh	*Cha, Col,* ***Eld, Gar****, Fen, Lem, Mar, Net, Sag, StJ*
Chilblains	*Ros*
Childrens' ills	*Cha, Mar, Mea*
Circulation	*Dan,* ***Gar, Gin****, Haw, Lem,* ***Ros,*** *Wil*

Colds ***Eld***, ***Gar***, *Lem*, ***Yar***
Cold limbs *Ros*
Colic *Cha*, ***Fen***
Colitis *Chi*, *Mar*, *Mea*
Congestion *Col*, *Sag*, *StJ*
Conjunctivitis ***Cha***, *Fen*, ***Mar***
Constipation *Bra*, *Dan*, *Fen*, *Row*
Coughs *Chi*, ***Col***, *Eld*, *Fen*, *Hon*, *Lem*, *Thy*, *StJ*
Cramps (see *circulation*)
Cystitis *Cle*, *Col*, ***Dan***, *She*, *Sil*, ***Yar***
Dandruff *Cle*, ***Net***
Debility *Bra*, *Cha*, ***Cle***, ***Dan***, *Haw*, *Lav*, *Mar*, *Net*, ***Ros***
Depression *Lav*, *Lem*, *Ros*, *Sag*
Diarrhoea *Bra*, ***Cra***, ***Mea***, *Net*, *Sag*, *She*, *StJ*, *Yar*
Digestive problems *Cha*, *Chi*, *Cra*, *Fen*, ***Gar***, *Gin*, *Lem*, *Mar*, ***Mea***, *Ros*, *Sag*, *Thy*, *StJ*, *Hop*
Draws out poisons & splinters *Chi*, ***Haw***
Dysentery *Lem*, *Net*, *StJ*
Ear infections *Cha*, ***Gar***, *Mar*, ***Thy***, *Yar*
Eczema ***Chi***, ***Cle***, ***Net***
Exhaustion *Lav*
Eye infections *Cha*, *Fen*, *Mar*
Eyes *Eld*, *Fen*
Fever *Cha*, *Eld*, *Gar*, *Lem*, ***Mea***, *Sag*, *Thy*, ***Yar***
Fibrosis *Ros*, *StJ*
Flatulence *Cha*, ***Fen***, *Lav*, *Lem*, *Ros*, *Thy*
Food poisoning *Fen*
Fungal infection ***Gar***, ***Mar***, *Sag*
Gall bladder ***Dan***, *Mar*
Gastritis *Cha*, ***Mea***
Glands (see too Lymph) ***Cle***, *Mar*
Gums *Bra*, *Cha*, *Lav*, *Sag*
Haemorrhage ***Yar***, ***She***
Haemorrhoids *Dan*, *Thy*
Hair tonic *Cle*, *Net*, *Ros*, *Sag*
Hangover *Thy*
Hard swellings *Cha*, *Thy*
Hay fever *Eld*, *Gar*
Headaches *Cha*, *Hon*, *Lav*, *Mea*, *Hop*, *Lem*, *Ros*, *Sag*, *Wil*
Heart problems *Dan*, *Gar*, *Hon*, ***Haw***, *Lav*, *Lem*, *Ros*, *Sag*
Heartburn ***Mea***, *Lem*
Heatrash *Chi*
Hot flushes *Lav*, *Lem*, *Sag*
Indigestion ***Cha***, ***Fen***, *Lin*, *Mea*, *Hop*
Immune system ***Cle***, ***Mar***, *Mea*
Infections ***Cle***, *Dan*, ***Gar***, *Sag*, *Thy*
Infectious diseases (kids) ***Mea***
Inflammations *Cha*, *Cle*, *Col*, *Hop*, *Mar*, *Mea*, *Sag*, *StJ*
Influenza *Lem*, *Eld*, ***Gar***, *Yar*
Insect bites & stings *Col*, *Dan*, *Lav* *Lem*, *Mar*, *Ros*, *Sag*
Insecticide ***Eld***, *Ros*
Insomnia ***Cha***, *Cle*, *Eld*, *Haw* *Hop*, *Lav*, *Lem*, *Thy*, *StJ*
Itching *Cha*, ***Chi***, *Cle*, ***Mar***, ***StJ***
Jaundice *Dan*
Joint pains *Cha*, *Hon*, *Lav*, ***Net***, *Thy*
Kidneys ***Dan***, *Mea*, *Sag*, *Thy*, *Hop*
Laryngitis ***Col***, *Sag*, ***Thy***
Liver problems ***Dan***, *Hon*, *Lav*, ***Mar***, *Mea*, *Ros*, *Sag*, *Thy*

Lung problems *Chi,* ***Col****, Fen,* ***Gar****, Hon, Sag, Thy*
Lymph cleanser ***Cle****, Dan,* ***Net***
Menopause *Lav, Lem, Sag, StJ*
Menstruation *Cha, Gin, Mar, Lem, Sag, She, Yar*
Milk (mother's) *Fen, Net, Sag*
Mouth Ulcers *Cha, Lav, Lem, Mar, Net, Sag*
Mucous membranes ***Cle****, Eld*
Mumps ***Cle****, Mea*
Muscle pain *Dan, Net, Ros, Thy*
Nausea ***Cha****, Fen, Lav,* ***Mea***
Nervous system *Haw, Lav, Lem, Lin, Ros, StJ, Thy*
Neuralgia *Mar, Ros, StJ*
Nosebleeds *Mar, Net, She, Yar*
Obesity *Chi, Fen, Mea*
Palpitations ***Haw****, Lav, Lem, Lin*
Phlegm *Col, Com, Eld,* ***Fen****, Net, Sag, StJ, Thy*
Pregnancy *Cha, Fen, Lem, Net (not safe: Mar, Ros, Sag)*
Psoriasis *Chi,* ***Cle***
Respiratory problems *(see Lung)*
Rheumatism *Chi, Com, Cra, Dan, Fen, Gar, Hon, Lav,* ***Mea****,* ***Net****, StJ, Sil, Thy,* ***Yar***
Scalp *Bra, Thy*
Sciatica *Ros, StJ, Thy*
Sedative *Eld, Hop, Lav, Mea, StJ, Hop*
Shock *Mar*
Sinusitis *Cha,* ***Eld****,* ***Gar****, Yar*
Skin problems *Bra, Cha, Chi, Cle, Col, Eld, Hon, StJ, Hop*
Sores *Ald, Chi, Hon, Hop*
Sore throat *Cha, Mar, Row,* ***Sag****, Sel, Thy, Wil*
Sprains *Com, Eld, Mar*
Spring Tonics *Cle, Eld, Net*
Stress *Haw, Hop, Lav, Lem, Lin, Ros, StJ*
Sunburn *Lav, Mar, StJ*
Sunstroke *Lav*
Tension *Hon, Hop, Lin, Hop*
Throat *Cha, Cle, Col, Sag, Thy*
Thrush ***Gar****,* ***Mar****, She, Thy*
Tonsillitis *Cle, Col, Gar, Sag, Thy*
Toothache *Cha, Lav, Mar, Yar, Hop*
Travel sickness *Lav*
Ulcers (mouth) *Cha, Lav, Mar, Sag, Sel, Wil*
Ulcers (skin) ***Cle****, Col, Hon, Hop,* ***Mar****, Sag, StJ, Yar*
Ulcers (stomach) *Chi, Dan, Mar,* ***Mea***
Urinary infection *Cle,* ***Dan****, Mea, Net, Yar*
Vaginal infection *Lem, Mar*
Varicose veins ***Dan****,* ***Haw****, Mar, StJ*
Viral infections ***Cle****, Dan, Gar, Mar*
Vomiting *Lav,* ***Mea****, Ros*
Warts *Dan*
Water retention *Cle,* ***Dan****, Gin, Hon, Mea, Net,* ***Yar***
Whooping cough *Col, Gar*
Wounds *Bla, Cha, Chi, Com, Eld, Gar, Hon, Hop,* ***Mar****, Net, Rob, Ros, Sag, Sel, She, StJ, Yar*